Companion to English Communication

大学生のための英語コミュニケーション入門

Esther WAER

DA Masakatsu

MA Hiroyuki

JN022634

NAN'UN-DO

FOREWORD by the authors

With the whole world connecting instantly via the internet, the importance of a common language is more important than ever. To be able to connect and communicate effectively with ease in English is a valuable skill for both business and pleasure. This requires not only a knowledge of grammar and a broad vocabulary, but also confidence and the ability to express yourself clearly. This book will help you feel more confident speaking English by focusing on simple and practical conversations in situations that you are familiar with.

People who learn English the quickest are often those who have something they want to say. High interest topics have been chosen which will let you talk about your own experiences and learn more about your classmates. This will make the classroom not just a place to learn a language but also an opportunity to learn more about yourself and connect with other students in an enjoyable way, while acquiring valuable skills in English useful for life and study. Topics such as how to organize time, discussion about daily habits and routines will offer insights into each other's lives and also allow you to share your experiences and tips for how to do things better.

Each unit begins with a short dialogue including useful expressions, and an example of how the target grammar point is used naturally in daily conversational English. With an emphasis on active learning, this is followed by questions to ask other students in the class. The reading section aims to address an aspect of daily life while introducing a new angle to stimulate thought and discussion. The essay is followed by comprehension questions to check you have understood the passage. There is a small writing activity, where you will have time to gather your thoughts, look up new words and try writing about your experiences. This is a quiet time to prepare for final part of the lesson: the discussion section. This is where you can talk more in depth about the topic and share your ideas. It may seem difficult at first, but it will get easier as you work through the book.

Finally, we hope that this textbook can help create an enjoyable and enriching experience in the classroom. After all, learning should be fun, and building new relationships is at the core of English communication. This textbook can be studied independently and is even better when paired with Companion to TOEIC Bridge for a complete course.

Table of Contents

Read by
Emma Howard
Chris Koprowski

Unit 1
Friends

Grammar Target: Present Tense

Activity 1   DIALOGUE   02

Listen and Repeat.

Clive: Hello, are you in Mr. William's art history class, too?

Anna: Yes, I am. It's a great class, isn't it?

Clive: Yes. I really like it. I'm Clive, nice to meet you.

Anna: I'm Anna, nice to meet you, too.

Clive: I'm new to this area. Do you know a good place for lunch?

Anna: I'm new, too. But, I heard the Blue Star café is good. I'm going now.
    Would you like to join me?

Clive: That would be great, thanks!

Activity 2   In-Class Activity: WARM-UP

Ask your partner the following questions.

Do you ever feel lonely?

What do you do if you feel lonely?

Do you find it easy to talk to new people?

What do you think is a good way to start a conversation with a stranger?

Do you ever feel lonely? Most people sometimes feel lonely. It's very normal. There are many reasons why people feel lonely such as: moving to a new area, working from home, being out of work, not feeling very well, or the death of a close friend or family member. A survey called the BBC Loneliness Experiment, which was answered by 55,000 people, found that 27% of people over 75 years old and 40% of 16-24 year-olds often feel lonely.

Even though loneliness is an unpleasant feeling, 41% of respondents thought that loneliness can be positive. It can prompt someone to go out and connect with people, find new things to do, or make time to think deeply. Some people said because of a lonely time in their lives they read many good books, or discovered a new hobby.

The survey also reports ways people help themselves to feel less lonely. The first was to find something to do, something that absorbs you. Other ideas included joining a club, starting a new hobby, changing the way you think, or chatting with people in shops and parks.

In response to this survey, one lady decided to do something to help people and opened a conversation café. She distributed fliers, and on the first day nervously waited to see if anyone would join. Many different kinds of people of all ages came. She made question sheets to help people start talking and soon the room was full of lively conversation. She hopes more conversation cafes will start around the U.K. to help lonely people.

Activity 4 VOCABULARY QUIZ

Find the right word from the essay that matches each definition below.

(1) not far from someone or something   (   )
(2) to interest someone so much   (   )
(3) to share things among a group of people   (   )
(4) a reaction to something that has happened or been said (   )
(5) to talk in a friendly way   (   )

Activity 5 TRUE or FALSE QUESTIONS

Read the sentences and check true or false.

(1) It's natural for people to feel lonely.   (   )
(2) Loneliness prevents you from thinking deeply.   (   )
(3) Quite a few people came to the conversation café. (   )

Activity 6 COMPREHENSION CHECK QUESTIONS

(1) Why can loneliness be positive?

_____

(2) What did a lonely time make some people do?

_____

(3) What did the woman do to help her customers start conversations?

_____

Activity 7 WRITING

Write about what you do if you feel lonely.

_____
_____
_____
_____
_____
_____
_____

(1) Do you prefer to have many friends or just a few very close friends?

_____

_____

_____

_____

(2) Think of five ways to meet new people.

_____

_____

_____

_____

(3) Discuss and decide the best three ways to make friends.

_____

_____

_____

_____

Unit 2
Hobbies

Grammar Target: Infinitive and Gerund, Adverbs of Frequency

Activity 1 DIALOGUE 04

Listen and repeat.

Chisato: What do you like doing in your free time?

George: I like running.

Chisato: How often do you run?

George: Almost every day. How about you? What do you like doing?

Chisato: I don't like exercising at all. I love going to the movies.

George: What kind of movies do you like?

Chisato: Anything except horror. I can't stand watching horror movies! How about you?

George: I don't watch movies very often. But I do enjoy watching science documentaries.

Activity 2 In-Class Activity: WARM-UP

Ask your partner the following questions.

What do you like doing in your free time?

What do you hate to do?

What do you like to do in winter?

A hobby is an activity people do regularly for pleasure, not for pay. It seems that people all over the world enjoy doing similar things. The most popular hobbies are reading, watching TV or movies, and listening to music.

However, not all hobbies are equal. There are high-value and low-value activities. Low-value hobbies are more passive, a way to pass time, such as watching TV, playing video games or surfing the Internet. Whereas high-value hobbies are more active. They have meaning and often involve learning a new skill or creating something. High-value hobbies are important as they add interest and enjoyment to people's lives away from work and household chores. They can be a topic of conversation, and can increase your social circle with people with the same interests. They give a feeling of satisfaction and achievement.

Occasionally, people's hobbies turn into paid work. For many, this can be a dream come true, to get paid to do what you love doing. These people say that they work more hours than a regular job, but that it is more satisfying. However, the downside is that they no longer have an activity to enjoy in their free time. In fact, one of the problems of turning a hobby into a job is that there is no clear time when work finishes. The hobby they once enjoyed can even become a source of stress. But most say that they still enjoy their work.

Activity 4   VOCABULARY QUIZ

Find the right word from the essay that matches each definition below.

(1) to give someone money for a product on a service   (   )
(2) the same in size, number, amount, or value   (   )
(3) a small job that you have to do regularly in the home   (   )
(4) sometimes, but not regularly, not often   (   )
(5) the negative part or disadvantage of something   (   )

Activity 5   TRUE or FALSE QUESTIONS

Read the sentences and check true or false.

(1) Hobbies can vary according to the regions people live.   (   )
(2) High-value hobbies often involve your work and household chores.   (   )
(3) Making your hobby a paid job can sometimes be stressful.   (   )

Activity 6   COMPREHENSION CHECK QUESTIONS

(1) What are the most popular hobbies?

_____

(2) What do high-value hobbies often involve?

_____

(3) Why are high-value hobbies important?

_____

Activity 7   WRITING

Write about things you like, love, enjoy, don't like, can't stand doing in your free time. Give reasons why.

_____
_____
_____
_____
_____
_____

(1) What do you like doing to relax?

_____

_____

_____

_____

_____

(2) What do you think are the benefits of having a hobby?

_____

_____

(3) What are your hobbies? Are they high or low value?

_____

_____

(4) Would you like your hobby to also be your job? Why? Why not?

_____

_____

Unit 3
Commuting

Grammar Target: How Questions

Listen and Repeat.

Tetsuo: Sorry, I'm late. I got stuck in traffic on the bypass. There was a bad accident.

Rachel: No problem. I stopped driving to work. The roads are so congested. It was too stressful.

Tetsuo: So how do you come to work now?

Rachel: I ride my bicycle. It's not too far. It only takes 30 minutes. It's good exercise.

Tetsuo: That sounds like hard work. Driving is so much more convenient.

Rachel: Not really. I feel great riding my bike and I see more of the city. When it rains, I catch the train, and I can relax and read a novel.

Activity 2   In-Class Activity: WARM-UP

Ask your partners the following questions.

How do you come to school?

How long does it take?

How far is your commute?

Can you think of one thing you like and one thing you don't like about your commute?

Do you enjoy your commute? Or is it something you dread every morning? Long commutes are said to increase stress and decrease health. According to a recent survey, people in Israel have the longest commute time at 97 minutes, the shortest average time is Japan with only 39 minutes.

5 In London the average commute is 74 minutes, the trains are crowded and expensive, the roads are congested with traffic jams, and petrol and parking are expensive. Most journeys are not very far. So why don't more people cycle? In fact, the number of commuters cycling to work in London has doubled in the last ten years. But still only 5% of all trips in the UK are made by bicycle, 10 compared to 30% in the Netherlands. Cycling is a great form of exercise and can keep people healthy; it can also improve your mood, memory and creative thinking, too.

However, some people say they enjoy their commute. They say it gives time for themselves, a neutral space in between home and work. Many people enjoy 15 reading novels, catching up on the news or listening to podcasts, maybe even taking a course to learn new skills. Others like to listen to music or podcasts in the privacy of their cars and enjoy time alone. Even so, being stuck in traffic can be tiring. And when trains are late or crowded, it can be stressful.

Activity 4   VOCABULARY QUIZ

Find the right word from the essay that matches each definition below.

(1) a place that is full of people   (   )
(2) a kind of a state that does not have any effect   (   )
(3) a long written story about imaginary people and events   (   )
(4) the knowledge or and ability that enables you to do something well

                                                                              (   )
(5) a way to say you are not looking forward to something   (   )

Activity 5   TRUE or FALSE QUESTIONS

Read the sentences and check true or false.

(1) In Japan, the average time to commute is less than half an hour.   (   )
(2) As many people in the UK commute by bike as people in Israel.   (   )
(3) Those who enjoy their commute consider it a nice private time.   (   )

Activity 6   COMPREHENSION CHECK QUESTIONS

(1) How long is the average commute time in London?

_____

(2) What can improve your memory?

_____

(3) What does the commute give people?

_____

Activity 7   WRITING

Write about your morning commute. How do you come, how far is it? Do you enjoy it? What do you see or do? What do you think about? Try to be as descriptive as possible and use your dictionary.

_____
_____
_____
_____
_____

Activity 8   DISCUSSION

(1) Which is the best way for you to commute?
Train, car, bus, bicycle, on foot, scooter.
Put in order of preference.

1 _____

2 _____

3 _____

(2) In pairs, please think of advantages and disadvantages for each method of transport. What does your partner think?

1 _____

2 _____

3 _____

(3) Next, discuss your order and try to persuade each other until you can agree on the best way to travel to work or school.

_____

Present your combined list with reasons to another pair. Ask each other questions.

_____

Unit 4
Fashion

Grammar Target: Present Continuous

Activity 1   DIALOGUE 08

Listen and Repeat.

Jane: Wow! Why are you wearing a suit?

Peter: I have a job interview after class. How do I look?

Jane: Very professional. What is the interview for?

Peter: It's for a job at an advertising company. What do you think about my tie?

Jane: It's really nice. It suits you.

Peter: Thanks. I was worried it was too colorful.

Jane: It's perfect for an advertising company interview. First impressions are important!

Activity 2   In-Class Activity: WARM-UP

Ask your partner the following questions.

What are you wearing today?

Why did you choose these clothes today?

Where do you buy your clothes?

How often do you buy clothes?

It can be said that clothes are the most powerful form of visual communication. Some even say that clothing is a form of art. It is art you can wear, mixing colors, textures, and styles. Some people argue it doesn't matter what you look like, that what you do is more important. However, most people agree that what you wear says a lot about you. The colors and style you choose send a message to those around. Even if you aren't interested in clothes, that is a message, too.

What we wear affects how we think, feel and behave and also how others react to us. Research has shown that wearing professional business clothes helps people think and negotiate better, and to feel more confident, whereas casual clothes help people to be friendlier, more creative and relaxed. Also the colors we choose give a message. For example, blue is said to give a message of confidence and reliability. Black sends a message of seriousness and intelligence. Red is the color to wear if you want to impress someone. It shows passion and power. Green brings a feeling of peace and contentment.

Companies and schools use the power of clothes in uniforms. In schools uniforms are said to give students a sense of identity and may even help students to concentrate on their work. Companies use uniforms to give a professional image and let customers know they can trust their employees.

Activity 4   VOCABULARY QUIZ

Find the right word from the essay that matches each definition below.

(1) in seeing, or received through sight   (   )

(2) the way a fabric feels to the touch   (   )

(3) to try to reach an agreement by discussion   (   )

(4) to act, or react   (   )

(5) a feeling of quiet happiness and satisfaction   (   )

Activity 5   TRUE or FALSE QUESTIONS

Read the sentences and check true or false.

(1) Your clothes seldom express yourself.   (   )

(2) Clothes have an effect on both the wearer and the people around. (   )

(3) Red clothes give a peaceful feeling.   (   )

Activity 6   COMPREHENSION CHECK QUESTIONS

(1) Why don't some people care about their clothes?

_____

(2) What color should you wear if you want to show you're intelligent?

_____

(3) What do companies use uniforms for?

_____

Activity 7   WRITING

Write in detail what you are wearing today and how it makes you feel. Use your dictionary.

_____

_____

_____

_____

_____

(1) Are you interested in clothes?

_____

_____

(2) What kind of style do you like?

_____

_____

(3) Do you think clothes are important?

_____

_____

(4) What do you think about uniforms?

_____

_____

Unit 5
Personality

Grammar Target: Comparative and Superlative

Activity 1   DIALOGUE 10

Listen and Repeat.

Dan: How did you do in the French speaking test?

Sue: Terrible. It's my worst subject. I get too nervous and forget everything!

Dan: Oh that's too bad. For me, the speaking section is much easier than the reading section.

Sue: Both are difficult for me. History is much easier, and more interesting.

Dan: Really? History is the most boring lesson for me. I like math better.

Sue: Math is too difficult. We should help each other study!

Activity 2   In-Class Activity: WARM-UP

Ask your partner the following questions.

What was your favorite lesson in high school? Why?

What lesson did you like the least? Why?

Which is easier for you, math or history?

Education has been changing. Students used to sit in rows, quietly, listening to the teacher and then writing assignments. However, classrooms have changed. Students discuss ideas in groups and learn through doing activities and projects. This has made lessons more interactive and enjoyable for many students. But not all people learn in the same way. There are many different personalities in a classroom. One important type is that of the introvert or extrovert.

Are you an introvert or an extrovert? Do you know what these words mean? Some people think that introverts are shy or don't like people and that extroverts are friendlier. However, that is not true. An easy way to understand these two personality types is that introverts recharge their energy by spending time alone, whereas extroverts get energy from other people. In fact, most of us are a mix of both types.

Introverts work well alone. They need time and space to think. They are good at individual research. If there are too many people, or if there is too much noise, they may not learn anything. Extroverts, on the other hand, enjoy talking and being with people. They learn better from discussion, and find quiet time alone very difficult.

If we are aware of different personality types and try to accept everyone's differences, lessons can be more enjoyable for everyone. Discussions and participation activities need to be balanced with quiet thinking and writing time. Is it easier for you to learn in a group or alone?

Activity 4   VOCABULARY QUIZ

Find the right word from the essay that matches each definition below.

(1) a piece of work that is given to someone as part of his or her job

(   )

(2) someone's character   (   )

(3) nervous about meeting or speaking to other people   (   )

(4) particular combination of things   (   )

(5) to take something that someone offers you   (   )

Activity 5   TRUE or FALSE QUESTIONS

Read the sentences and check true or false.

(1) Sitting in rows has made classrooms more enjoyable.   (   )

(2) Extroverts need more time alone than introverts.   (   )

(3) Introverts find it more difficult to be with others when learning. (   )

Activity 6   COMPREHENSION CHECK QUESTIONS

(1) What has made lessons more interactive and enjoyable?

_____

(2) Where do extroverts get energy from?

_____

(3) What are introverts good at?

_____

Activity 7   WRITING

Write about what kind of person you are.
Are you shy, friendly, talkative, quiet, serious, kind, nervous, relaxed?
Use your dictionary to find the words you would like to use.

_____

_____

_____

_____

(1) Do you think studying alone or with friends is more effective?

_____

_____

_____

_____

(2) What style of lesson do you like best? Why?

_____

_____

_____

(3) Are you more introverted or extroverted? Why do you think so?

_____

_____

_____

_____

Unit 6
Sleep

Grammar Target: Prepositions of Time

Activity 1   DIALOGUE 12

Listen and Repeat.

Sarah: Good morning! How are you?

Robin: Not so good. I'm really tired today.

Sarah: You do look tired! What time did you go to bed last night?

Robin: At around 11:30, the same time as usual.

Sarah: What time did you wake up?

Robin: At 7, but I don't think I slept well. I had lots of strange dreams.

Sarah: What did you do before going to bed?

Robin: Nothing special. But I think I drank too much coffee.

Activity 2   In-Class Activity: WARM-UP

Ask your partner the following questions.

What do you do before going to sleep?
What time do you usually go to bed?
What time do you wake up?
Do you think you get enough sleep?

In modern society, sleeping less is often a sign of being a hard worker. As the pace of life gets faster, people are working more, staying up later, and sleeping less. Insomnia is a growing problem. In the U.K. in 1942 only 8% of the population slept less than six hours a night, but in 2017 almost 50% of people were. The U.K. still has an average sleeping time per person of 7 hours 30 minutes, New Zealand has the longest with 7 hours 50 minutes, and Japan has the least sleep with an average of 6 hours 15 minutes.

However, researchers are warning that sleeping is much more important than most people think and recommend that people sleep for at least 7 hours a night. Research shows that sleeping enough can protect us from many diseases and that the brain cleans itself during sleep. Also after only one night of four or five hours sleep, immune function drops by 70%. Lack of sleep is also linked to depression and anxiety.

So, if you want a healthy body and brain, sleeping 8 hours every night is essential. What do you need to do if you can't sleep? Make sure to exercise during the day. Stop watching TV or using your phone two hours before bed. Try to relax in the evening by listening to music, reading a book, or doing meditation. Take a hot bath before bed. Make sure your room is dark and quiet; maybe use earplugs and an eye mask. What is your bed time routine?

Activity 4   VOCABULARY QUIZ

Find the right word from the essay that matches each definition below.

(1) a condition where people can't sleep   (   )
(2) the number of people in a country   (   )
(3) to inform about a present or future danger   (   )
(4) the practice of emptying your mind of thoughts   (   )
(5) a series of actions performed regularly in the same way (   )

Activity 5   TRUE or FALSE QUESTIONS

Read the sentences and check true or false.

(1) People in the U.K. sleep more than people in Japan.   (   )
(2) Modern people sleep more than they used to.   (   )
(3) Sleeping for less than 7 hours is healthy.   (   )

Activity 6   COMPREHENSION CHECK QUESTIONS

(1) What does sleeping less often stand for in modern society?

_____

(2) How long do researchers recommend people to sleep?

_____

(3) What should people stop two hours before bed?

_____

Activity 7   WRITING

(1) Write about your bedtime routine using the words, first, then, next, finally.

_____
_____
_____
_____

(2) Present this to your partner. Ask each other questions.

Ask each other the questions below. Take time to think about your own answers first.

(1) Are you a night owl or a morning lark?

_____

(2) How many hours do you sleep every night?

_____

(3) Do you sleep well?

_____

(4) What do you do before you go to bed?

_____

(5) What do you do in the morning?

_____

(6) Do you have a lot of dreams?

_____

(7) Have you ever had a nightmare?

_____

_____

_____

Unit 7
Travel

Grammar Target: Future Tense

Activity 1   DIALOGUE 14

Listen and Repeat.

> **Tim:** What are you going to do this summer vacation?
>
> **Dawn:** I'm going to go to Thailand.
>
> **Tim:** That sounds like fun! Who are you going to go with?
>
> **Dawn:** No one, I'm going by myself.
>
> **Tim:** Really? Isn't it dangerous?
>
> **Dawn:** No, not at all. I often travel alone. It's fun and people are helpful.
>
> **Tim:** Don't you get lonely?
>
> **Dawn:** No, travelling alone is a great way to meet new people.

Activity 2   In-Class Activity: WARM-UP

Ask your partner the following questions.

What are you going to eat for dinner tonight?
What are you going to do this weekend?
Do you like travelling? Why? Why not?

Why do people travel? It can be for many different reasons. Some people travel to relax in a beautiful place with friends or family, to escape from daily life. Others want excitement, an adventure, to see new places and try new things. For some it's a time to enjoy eating new foods and shopping.

5 Whatever the reason for travelling, it's a way to have different experiences and to see how other people around the world live. We can learn about other cultures and religions which can help us understand our own country better. Some doctors also say that being in a new environment makes your brain healthy because you use your senses and have to observe many things which 10 sharpens your mind. Research has also shown that people were more creative after travelling overseas, and could generate more ideas.

Finally, which is better to travel alone or with friends? If you travel alone, you can go where you want when you want. You don't need to think about what other people want to do. It's easier to meet people too. Also, you have more 15 time to think and learn about yourself. Although travelling with friends is a lot of fun and you can help each other. You can share the experience, and make lifelong memories together.

However, some people find travelling stressful and expensive and much prefer to stay home and learn about the world through books and TV. How 20 about you?

Activity 4   VOCABULARY QUIZ

Find the right word from the essay that matches each definition below.

(1) to get away, to leave a place when something tries to catch you

(   )

(2) knowledge or skill that you gain from doing something   (   )

(3) a belief in one or more gods   (   )

(4) involving the use of imagination to produce new ideas   (   )

(5) to cause or produce something   (   )

Activity 5   TRUE or FALSE QUESTIONS

Read the sentences and check true or false.

(1) Learning other cultures can help you understand religions.   (   )

(2) Travelling alone is a way to let others do what they want.   (   )

(3) Those who prefer to stay at home think traveling costs too much. (   )

Activity 6   COMPREHENSION CHECK QUESTIONS

(1) What makes your brain healthy?

_____

(2) What can you expect after travelling overseas?

_____

(3) What can you make by travelling with friends?

_____

Activity 7   WRITING

Write about your plans for this weekend, using 'going to'.

_____

_____

_____

_____

_____

(1) What do you think the benefits of travel are?

_____

_____

(2) What are the disadvantages of travelling overseas?

_____

_____

(3) Do you prefer to travel alone or with a friend?

_____

_____

(4) What are you going to do on your next vacation?

_____

_____

Unit 8
Diets

Grammar Target: Present Perfect Tense

Activity 1   DIALOGUE 16

Listen and Repeat.

Jill: Good morning! Do you want to try that new café?

Lucy: Sure, let's!

Jill: Have you eaten breakfast yet? The vegetarian special is really good.

Lucy: Oh, I've already eaten. I'll just have a coffee.

Jill: I overslept. So I haven't eaten anything! I'm starving!

Activity 2   In-Class Activity: WARM-UP

Ask your partner the following questions.

What do you like to eat for breakfast?

What is your favorite food?

Do you like cooking?

What kind of food do you cook?

It is said that cooking and sharing food is what makes us human. It is an important part of life, not just for survival but for pleasure and socializing, too. There are many different styles of eating and many opinions on which is the healthiest.

⁵ The number of people who are following a vegan diet is increasing steadily. A vegan is someone who doesn't eat anything from animals, fish or seafood. This includes eggs, milk, and cheese. People say this is better for both the environment and people's health. But is it really healthy? Nutritionists say vegans need to be careful because important nutrients such as vitamin B12, ¹⁰ are mainly found in animal products. Some also say that vegans tend to rely on imported and processed food more.

The paleo diet takes its inspiration from human history. It is based on foods which humans may have eaten during the Paleolithic era about 2.5 million to 10,000 years ago. During this time humans didn't farm, they were hunter ¹⁵ gatherers. The diet includes meat, fish, fruit, vegetables, nuts and seeds, no dairy or grains such as rice or wheat. It is not a diet for bread lovers.

However, most experts agree that a flexitarian diet is best. It is mainly vegetarian but with small amounts of meat, fish and dairy. In fact, the traditional Japanese diet is a perfect example of this.

Activity 4   VOCABULARY QUIZ

Find the right word from the essay that matches each definition below.

(1) the state of continuing to live   (   )
(2) the kind of food that a person or animal eats each day   (   )
(3) the natural features of a place   (   )
(4) something in food necessary for life   (   )
(5) a period of time in history   (   )

Activity 5   TRUE or FALSE QUESTIONS

Read the sentences and check true or false.

(1) A vegan only sometimes eats cheese for health reasons.   (   )
(2) People started farming in the Paleolithic era.   (   )
(3) The traditional Japanese diet is considered a flexitarian.   (   )

Activity 6   COMPREHENSION CHECK QUESTIONS

(1) Why do vegans need to be careful?

_____

(2) What do vegans tend to rely on?

_____

(3) What did they eat during the Paleolithic period?

_____

Activity 7   WRITING

Write about the most delicious or worst meal you have ever eaten. Try to include information about where you ate it, who cooked it, if it was a special occasion, how you felt, who you were with.

_____
_____
_____
_____
_____

Activity 8   DISCUSSION

(1) Is your diet healthy? How could you eat more healthily?

_____

_____

_____

(2) Have you tried being vegan or vegetarian? Why? Why not?

_____

_____

_____

(3) What is the most delicious meal you have ever eaten?

_____

_____

_____

Unit 9
Money

Grammar Target: Auxiliary Verbs

Activity 1   DIALOGUE 🎧 18

Listen and Repeat.

Jim : Hey, do you want to go snowboarding in Hokkaido next week?
Rob : I'd love to, but I can't afford it this month.
Jim : I can lend you some money.
Rob : Thanks, but I'll get paid at the end of the month.
Jim : OK, how about next month?
Rob : That would be great!

Activity 2   In-Class Activity: WARM-UP

Ask your partner the following questions.

Do you have a part-time job?
What's the most expensive thing you have ever bought?
Have you ever borrowed money from a friend?

"Time is money" is an often-quoted phrase and means that time is valuable and shouldn't be wasted. We all know money is important, but it is not something people talk about very much. In many cultures, it is considered rude to talk about money. People say that a healthy relationship with money is a large
5 part of wellness. It may be as important to our well-being as are exercise, food, and sleep. In fact, money problems can be the biggest source of stress in life.

Financial well-being includes having low debt, being able to save money to meet goals, having an emergency fund for the unexpected, and being able to spend money in ways that have value for you. Some people like to spend
10 money on things, while other people like to spend on experiences. A few easy tips to increase financial well-being are limiting the use of credit cards, keeping track of how you spend your money, avoiding tempting situations, and most importantly spending less than you earn.

To help increase savings, it is good to set a budget for each month and to
15 try and save at least 20% of what you earn. Some people have separate bank accounts—one for daily expenses and another for saving. Keeping money in a savings account helps people to avoid using the money. Some people simply save coins in a jar.

Activity 4   VOCABULARY QUIZ

Find the right word from the essay that matches each definition below.

(1) worth a lot of money   (   )
(2) speaking or behaving in a way that is not polite   (   )
(3) a sum of money that a person or organization owes   (   )
(4) to prevent something bad from happening   (   )
(5) a plan of how the money will be spent   (   )

Activity 5   TRUE or FALSE QUESTIONS

Read the sentences and check true or false.

(1) It isn't polite to talk about money in some cultures.   (   )
(2) Using credit cards is good for financial health.   (   )
(3) Saving accounts help people spend less money.   (   )

Activity 6   COMPREHENSION CHECK QUESTIONS

(1) Why should time be not wasted?

_____

(2) What is a large part of wellness?

_____

(3) How do some people avoid using money?

_____

Activity 7   WRITING

Write advice for a friend on how to save money. Try to use 'you should', 'you could', 'why don't you ...?'

_____
_____
_____
_____
_____

(1) Do you prefer to spend money on things or experiences?

_____

_____

(2) If you had to make a choice, would you rather work hard and have lots of money than work less and live simply?

_____

_____

_____

(3) What ideas do you have for saving money? Think of three and share with your group.

_____

_____

_____

Unit 10
E-books

Grammar Target: Inanimate Subject

Activity 1   DIALOGUE 20

Listen and Repeat.

Jane: Did you see that new drama last night?

Linda: No, what is it about?

Jane: It's about a couple who became homeless and decided to hike around the U.K.

Linda: That makes me wonder... Where did they sleep?

Jane: In a tent. It's a true story. I've read the book. You should watch it.

Linda: It will interest my boyfriend a lot. We'll watch it together, thanks!

Activity 2   In-Class Activity: WARM-UP

Ask your partner the following questions.

Which do you prefer, watching TV or reading? Why?

How often do you read novels?

Have you bought a book recently?

When e-books were first sold in shops, some people predicted that it was the end for paper books. After all, with one e-book you can carry thousands of books and have the ability to buy more books instantly wherever you are. E-books usually have inbuilt dictionaries so you can look up new words. You can also make notes and save quotes. E-books are easier for older people and people with weak eyesight to read because of the backlight and the ability to change the text size.

However, people haven't given up paper books yet. In the last few years, sales of e-books have been declining while sales of paper books have been increasing. One disadvantage of e-books is that of screen fatigue. People are spending more time in front of computers, so paper books may be more relaxing. Also, if you enjoyed your book, you can easily lend it to a friend.

No matter which format you choose to use, reading can improve your imagination, your vocabulary, and help make you a better writer. Studies have shown that reading books is better for people than watching TV. When you read, you concentrate and use your imagination more, but watching TV is passive. Brain scans have shown that reading increases activity in the brain, and suggests that readers experience similar feelings as the characters in the book. Research has shown that reading also calms nerves and reduces stress even more than listening to music. What are you going to read next?

Activity 4   VOCABULARY QUIZ

Find the right word from the essay that matches each definition below.

(1) to say something that will happen, before it happens   (   )

(2) to hold something in your hand as you take it somewhere   (   )

(3) to repeat exactly what someone else has said or written   (   )

(4) extreme tiredness   (   )

(5) to make someone become quiet and relaxed   (   )

Activity 5   TRUE or FALSE QUESTIONS

Read the sentences and check true or false.

(1) People thought that paper books would decline in the future.   (   )

(2) E-books enable readers to protect their eyes.   (   )

(3) Brain scans found that brain activity increased when reading. (   )

Activity 6   COMPREHENSION CHECK QUESTIONS

(1) What can e-books enable you to do?

_____

(2) What happened to the sales of e-books in the last few years?

_____

(3) What does reading make readers experience?

_____

Activity 7   WRITING

Write about an interesting TV program or book that you have seen or read recently. Tell us what it was about and why you liked it. What did you learn from it?

_____

_____

_____

_____

_____

_____

(1) What kind of books do you enjoy reading?

_____

_____

_____

(2) What have you read recently? What was it about?

_____

_____

_____

(3) Do you read paper books or e-books? List the advantages and disadvantages of both.

_____

_____

_____

Grammar Target: Reported Speech

Activity 1   DIALOGUE   22

Listen and Repeat.

Riley: Oh, I'm a bit nervous.

Megan: Why?

Riley: Well, last night I asked my online friend if she would meet me in real life.

Megan: Really? What did she say?

Riley: She said that she would love to.

Megan: That's great, isn't it?

Riley: Yeah. But we get on so well online, what if we don't like each other when we meet?

Megan: Oh, I'm sure you will!

Activity 2   In-Class Activity: WARM-UP

Ask your partner the following questions.

What kind of phone do you have?

How many hours a day do you spend on your phone?

What app do you use the most?

Smart phones have changed the way we socialize. In the U.S. smart phone usage grew from 35% in 2011 to 81% in 2019. Social media usage increased from 50% in 2011 to 79% in 2019. The average American spends around six hours a day on their smart phones. It's not surprising that online friends are a large part of modern life. Often online friends have never met in real life. However, people report that these friendships can be just as close as real-life friendships.

Is it possible to fall in love with a person you've never met? Apparently so. In fact, it is now the second most popular way to meet someone. The most popular way is through friends. Experts suggest that relationships made online can be stronger. Perhaps this is because it brings together people who share similar interests and beliefs, even if they live far apart. Also, anonymous online interactions are often deeper and more meaningful. Research suggests that not only is it possible to fall in love, but that divorce rates are lower among those who met online.

Why do these anonymous meetings create deeper relationships? A psychology experiment performed in 1973 called 'Deviance in the dark' may help explain. Participants were put in a totally dark room with people they didn't know and told they would not meet after leaving the room. The experiment showed that anonymity made people feel free and yet more serious. They were less inhibited and more willing to open up. However, there can be a darker side to anonymous online relationships. If you are falling in love online, do some research on the person and arrange a face-to-face meeting in a public place.

Activity 4　VOCABULARY QUIZ

Find the right word from the essay that matches each definition below.

(1) to spend with other people in a friendly way　　　(　　　　)
(2) unknown by name　　　　　　　　　　　　　　　(　　　　)
(3) the legal ending of a marriage　　　　　　　　　　(　　　　)
(4) the study of the mind and behavior　　　　　　　(　　　　)
(5) too embarrassed or nervous to do what you want　(　　　　)

Activity 5　TRUE or FALSE QUESTIONS

Read the sentences and check true or false.

(1) Online friends are common in modern society.　　　　　　(　　)
(2) Romance through online interaction seldom happens.　　　(　　)
(3) 'Deviance in the dark' is a good example of the result of online love.　(　　)

Activity 6　COMPREHENSION CHECK QUESTIONS

(1) What is the second most popular way to meet someone?

_____

(2) Why can relationships made online be stronger?

_____

(3) What should you do if you fall in love online?

_____

Activity 7　WRITING

Write about your favorite social media app and why you like it? If you don't have one, why don't you use social media?

_____

_____

_____

_____

_____

Activity 8   DISCUSSION

(1) How did your parents meet?

_____

_____

_____

(2) Do you have online friends you've never met in person? Do you think on-line friends can be 'true' friends?

_____

_____

_____

(3) What do you think are the advantages and disadvantages of online friends and communities?

_____

_____

_____

Unit 12
Productivity

Grammar Target: Adjectives and Adverbs

Activity 1   DIALOGUE   24

Listen and Repeat.

Julie: Hi. Have you finished your assignment?

Nikki: Yeah, I handed it in last week.

Julie: Wow, that was quick work! How did you do it? I'm working so slowly. I'm only halfway through.

Nikki: Actually, I studied methods to help me work quickly, and they worked!

Julie: Please tell me what you did.

Nikki: Sure, let's go for a coffee!

Activity 2   In-Class Activity: WARM-UP

Ask your partner the following questions.

Do you have a lot of assignments to do?

When do you work best? In the morning, afternoon, or evening?

Do you listen to music or watch TV while you study?

Can you concentrate and finish your work quickly? If the answer is no, you are not alone. Have you heard of Parkinson's Law? It is an observation that your work will expand to fill the time you have. In other words, if you have a week to finish a two-hour assignment, it will take you a week. There is a belief that the longer you spend on something, the better the quality of the work. However, it is not true if a lot of that time is wasted.

Productivity methods aim to help you work more effectively and get more done in less time. One method which helps to increase concentration and prevent fatigue is the Pomodoro Technique, which was developed by Francesco Cirillo in the 1980's. It is a time-management technique in which you work for 25 minutes and then take a break for 5 minutes. After four 25-minute blocks you take a longer break for 15 minutes. You can set a timer, or download an app. It works because the human brain can't focus on a single task for a long time. The breaks help reenergize your brain and improve the quality of your work.

Another technique is to make a list and prioritize the jobs that are most urgent. Focus on one job at a time. It has been proven that multitasking is less efficient because it involves the brain making rapid switches. This impairs focus and increases brain fatigue. In fact, studies show that when you switch tasks it can take 23 minutes to refocus! Make sure to turn off notifications on your phone so you are not interrupted.

Activity 4   VOCABULARY QUIZ

Find the right word from the essay that matches each definition below.

(1) the feeling that something is definitely true   (   )

(2) a planned way of doing something   (   )

(3) to put things in order of importance   (   )

(4) to damage something   (   )

(5) to stop someone from continuing what they are doing   (   )

Activity 5   TRUE or FALSE QUESTIONS

Read the sentences and check true or false.

(1) The more you spend time on your work, the better the quality.   (   )

(2) Pomodoro Technique can stop your brain from getting tired.   (   )

(3) Multitasking is one way to make you work more efficiently.   (   )

Activity 6   COMPREHENSION CHECK QUESTIONS

(1) What do the breaks in Pomodoro Technique help with?

_____

(2) How long does it take to refocus after switching tasks?

_____

(3) What do you need to do in order not to get interrupted?

_____

Activity 7   WRITING

Write about things you do to help you study better and more quickly.

_____

_____

_____

_____

_____

(1) Do you think you use your time well? Or, do you waste time? What do you waste time doing?

_____

_____

_____

(2) What interrupts or distracts you when you are working or studying?

_____

_____

_____

(3) What method do you use to study or complete assignments?

_____

_____

_____

Unit 13
Pets

Grammar Target: Prepositions of Place

Listen and Repeat.

> Gill: I'm so tired today. I couldn't sleep well last night.
>
> Paul: Why not?
>
> Gill: My dog kept waking me up!
>
> Paul: Does your dog sleep in your bed?
>
> Gill: No, he sleeps at the end of my bed, or outside my door.
>
> Paul: I wish I had a dog. I love taking dogs for walks.
>
> Gill: You can take mine anytime! He needs a lot of walking!

Activity 2   In-Class Activity: WARM-UP
Ask your partner the following questions.

What's your favorite animal?
Do you have a pet?
Which do you prefer, cats or dogs?

Archaeology suggests that humans have had dogs as pets for over 12,000 years. Even now dogs remain our most popular pet. A survey taken in 2018 reported that 11.5% of Japanese people have a dog and 10.1% have a cat. While in the U.K., 25% of people have a dog and 17% have a cat. Pets are often kept for companionship and are considered a member of the family. In fact, another survey in the U.K. reported that 12% of people said that they loved their pet more than their partner. Another 9% admitted to loving their pet more than their children!

Pets provide owners with emotional support. Studies have shown that stroking pets lowers heart rates and stress levels. Some scientists suggest that the bacteria pets bring into the house could reduce allergies in later life. Also, dogs keep their owners active and social, as many people say they often chat to other dog walkers. Other studies have shown that people with pets sleep better and visit the doctor less. However, this could be due to the fact that people who own pets are often wealthier.

The downside of keeping pets is that it can cost a lot of money if the animal gets sick. In the U.K. around 6,000 people go to hospital for dog bites. They can also bring fleas and diseases into the house. Another case against keeping pets is that, if people consider their pet to be part of the family, or a friend, a being with intelligence and emotions, then is it ethical to control their lives? What do you think about keeping pets?

Activity 4 VOCABULARY QUIZ

Find the right word from the essay that matches each definition below.

(1) to continue to be in the same state   (   )
(2) to move your hand gently over something   (   )
(3) having a lot of money   (   )
(4) the ability to learn, understand, and think   (   )
(5) relating to principles of what is right and wrong (   )

Activity 5 TRUE or FALSE QUESTIONS

Read the sentences and check true or false.

(1) One-third of pet owners love their pets more than their children.   (   )
(2) Touching pets could improve your health.   (   )
(3) It is illegal to control pets' lives.   (   )

Activity 6 COMPREHENSION CHECK QUESTIONS

(1) How many years have humans had dogs as pets?

_____

(2) What may the bacteria pets bring to the house do?

_____

(3) Why are dog owners active and social?

_____

Activity 7 WRITING

Do you have a pet? Write about your pet. Or write about what pet you would like, or why you don't want a pet.

_____

_____

_____

_____

_____

(1) What do you think is a good animal for a pet?
    List your reasons why.

    _____

    _____

    _____

(2) Do you think it's OK to keep pets? Write reasons for and against. Take sides
    and discuss with your partner.

    _____

    _____

    _____

(3) Imagine you and your partner are a couple trying to decide on what pet to
    get. Try to persuade each other to get the pet you want.

    _____

    _____

    _____

Unit 14
Made by Hand

Grammar Target: Passive Voice

Activity 1   DIALOGUE 28
Listen and Repeat.

Max: That's a cool bag!

Chris: Thanks, it's really useful. It has a lot of pockets. Perfect for holding everything I need.

Max: What make is it?

Chris: It isn't a brand bag. It's handmade.

Max: Really? Who made it?

Chris: It was made by my sister. It's made from upcycled sofa material.

Max: Can she make me one, too?

Chris: Sure, she has an online shop. Take a look!

Activity 2   In-Class Activity: WARM-UP
Ask your partner the following questions.

How often do you go shopping?

When shopping, which is more important, price or quality? Why?

Do you prefer to shop online or in real shops? Why?

In response to climate change, there is a gradual change in consumer behavior. People are starting to buy less, and to re-use or repair more in order to help the environment. People are trying to waste less. There is a resurgence of small businesses selling local handmade goods. This is a reaction against mass production and giant companies who place profit above the welfare of people and the environment.

The beginnings of this movement to buy handmade can be seen in an online Handmade Pledge that first appeared in October 2007, stating that 'I pledge to buy handmade this holiday season, and request that others do the same for me,' which was signed by thousands of people. This was started in order to encourage people to support small businesses and artists.

In 2005, two years before the pledge, an online marketplace for handmade goods, called Etsy, was launched. Etsy works as a platform between creators and buyers, and takes a small percentage of the sales price. It has continued to grow and expand every year. Etsy's revenue in 2012 was $74.6 million and grew to $603.7 million in 2018. These figures indicate that people want to buy handmade items directly from the makers.

Makers and buyers believe that supporting small local businesses and people who sell handmade items can be a political message or a form of activism. It is a way to change the world for the better through the choices made when shopping. Consumers hold power to make changes like these. How can you use your consumer power to make a positive change?

Activity 4   VOCABULARY QUIZ

Find the right word from the essay that matches each definition below.

(1) happening slowly   (   )
(2) extremely big   (   )
(3) one's health and happiness   (   )
(4) to make a formal promise   (   )
(5) to start something   (   )

Activity 5   TRUE or FALSE QUESTIONS

Read the sentences and check true or false.

(1) Local handmade goods have become popular again.   (   )
(2) Etsy is a virtual place where you can buy handmade items.   (   )
(3) Choosing what you buy can state your political message.   (   )

Activity 6   COMPREHENSION CHECK QUESTIONS

(1) What do large companies value most?

_____

(2) What was the main purpose of the Handmade Pledge?

_____

(3) What does the growth of Etsy suggest?

_____

Activity 7   WRITING

Write about something you own that you love. What is it used for? Who was it made or designed by? Where was it made? What is it made from?

_____

_____

_____

_____

_____

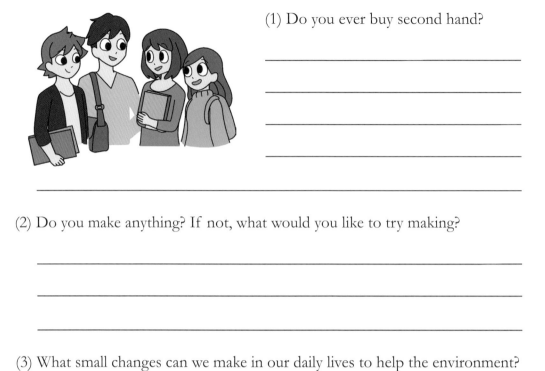

(1) Do you ever buy second hand?

_____

_____

_____

_____

_____

(2) Do you make anything? If not, what would you like to try making?

_____

_____

_____

(3) What small changes can we make in our daily lives to help the environment?

_____

_____

_____

Unit 15
Writing

Grammar Target: Conjunctions

Activity 1   DIALOGUE   30

Listen and Repeat.

Sarah: You look happy! What's up?

Luke: I just got a letter from my friend in France. It's so good to hear from him.

Sarah: Wow, I never get letters because I always email people. It's much easier.

Luke: Me, too, most of the time. But letters feel special. It's nice to hold the paper and see their handwriting.

Sarah: That's true. And it's fun to use pretty stationery, too.

Luke: I guess so. It's also more relaxed because you don't have to reply immediately.

Sarah: I think I'll write a letter to my friend today!

Activity 2   In-Class Activity: WARM-UP

Ask your partner the following questions.

Which are you faster at, writing by hand, or typing?

What is your favorite way to communicate with friends?

Do you prefer texting or calling?

The first signs of writing date back to 3,500 BCE, almost 30,000 years after language emerged. It seems that humans started writing in order to communicate across long distances for trade with earliest records listing numbers of beer jars. Early rulers were able to expand their power using
5   writing to give orders, make agreements, keep records, write history, and store knowledge. Of course, writing continues to be an essential skill in business. In fact, studies show that the three skills that employers value most in job candidates are leadership, team working, and writing skills.

   In this modern age of information, people are writing more than ever in
10 both their business and personal lives. Most people now chat with friends and family on apps rather than making phone calls. And e-mails are a large part of working life. Writing is an excellent way to conduct complex business negotiations that involve facts and figures. You can take time to compose the message, so there are fewer mistakes and misunderstandings and you can create
15 a permanent record to refer back to later. Good writing for business should be clear and succinct. Bad grammar or a lack of basic writing skills looks unprofessional.

   Interestingly, the way you choose to write can have different results. Typing is fast and easy to read. It is great for taking notes word for word, especially for
20 factual topics involving data. However, writing by hand forces the note taker to summarize and identify the important points. This involves more processing and a greater depth of understanding. Taking notes by hand also allows more freedom for creativity, which helps people remember and organize information more effectively.

Activity 4   VOCABULARY QUIZ

Find the right word from the essay that matches each definition below.

(1) to appear or come out from somewhere   (   )
(2) to think someone or something is important   (   )
(3) clearly expressed in a few words   (   )
(4) continuing to exist for a long time   (   )
(5) to recognize something correctly   (   )

Activity 5   TRUE or FALSE QUESTIONS

Read the sentences and check true or false.

(1) Writing helped early rulers become more powerful.   (   )
(2) Writing helps with difficult negotiations.   (   )
(3) Typing is better for summarizing than writing by hand.   (   )

Activity 6   COMPREHENSION CHECK QUESTIONS

(1) When did humans start writing?

_____

(2) How do most people chat these days?

_____

(3) What is taking notes by typing suitable for?

_____

Activity 7   WRITING

Write about why you prefer to write by hand or type. Give three reasons with explanations. Try to use 'so, because, or but.'

_____

_____

_____

_____

_____

(1) Do you ever write letters?

_____

_____

_____

(2) Why do people write journals?

_____

_____

_____

_____

(3) Do you prefer to take notes on a computer or by hand?

_____

_____

_____

Unit 16
Food Culture

Grammar Target: Relative Pronouns

Activity 1   DIALOGUE 32

Listen and Repeat.

Ren: Where do you live in London?

Andy: Let me show on this map. Here. This is the street that I live on.

Ren: What is this big green area?

Andy: That's a park where I used to play when I was a child.

Ren: What's it like to live in London?

Andy: It's really interesting. People from all over the world live in London, so you can learn a lot about other cultures. It's a great place to try different foods.

Ren: Sounds like fun. I want to visit one day!

Activity 2   In-Class Activity: WARM-UP

Ask your partner the following questions.

What foods from other countries are popular in Japan?

If you went to live in another country, what Japanese food would you take with you?

Do you think international exchange is important? Why? Why not?

Did you know that curry is one of the most popular foods in Britain? Some people say it is the new national dish. Although curry has its origins in India, there isn't actually a dish called 'curry' in India. The word 'curry' came from the Tamil word *kari*, which refers to a sauce for rice that uses the leaves of the curry tree. Many English people lived and worked in India, and they grew to like the spicy food. When they returned home, they still wanted to eat the food they had enjoyed in India. The first restaurant to put curry on its menu was Norris Street Coffee House in London in 1733.

However, it wasn't until the 1950s that curry really began to get popular in the U.K. In the beginning it was mainly sold in fish and chip shops. In 1971 many immigrants from Bangladesh came to live in the U.K., with many starting to work in the food industry. To this day around 70% of Indian restaurants are owned by people of Bangladeshi origin. It is said that there are more Indian restaurants in the London area than there are in Delhi and Mumbai combined. Surprisingly some British curries have now been exported back to India.

Japan shares its love of curry with the British, and reportedly eat curry more often than *sushi* or *tempura*. But did you know that the Japanese curry came to Japan not from India, but from Britain? It was introduced to Japan in the 1870s by the British Navy. The Japanese Navy starting feeding it to the sailors and it is still on the menu every Friday. Recently, Japanese curry has made its way to Britain and has quickly become a favorite.

Activity 4   VOCABULARY QUIZ

Find the right word from the essay that matches each definition below.

(1) the place in which something begins to exist   (   )

(2) related to a whole country   (   )

(3) someone who enters another country to live there permanently

(   )

(4) to have something which belongs to you   (   )

(5) a country's military force that fights at sea   (   )

Activity 5   TRUE or FALSE QUESTIONS

Read the sentences and check true or false.

(1) Curry is an Indian dish.   (   )

(2) Most Indian restaurants in England are operated by immigrants.   (   )

(3) Japanese people have curry more often than they have sushi.   (   )

Activity 6   COMPREHENSION CHECK QUESTIONS

(1) Where does the word 'curry' come from?

_____

(2) Where was curry mainly sold in England?

_____

(3) Which country introduced curry to Japan?

_____

Activity 7   WRITING

Would you like to live and work in another country? Write about where and why. Or write about why you don't want to.

_____

_____

_____

_____

(1) If you could try food from any country, which country would you choose?

_____

_____

_____

_____

_____

(2) If you were going to open a Japanese shop or restaurant overseas, what would you sell?

_____

_____

_____

(3) Would you like to live in multi-cultural cosmopolitan society? Why? Why not?

_____

_____

_____

Unit 17
Stress

Grammar Target: Conditional Mood

Activity 1   DIALOGUE 34

Listen and Repeat.

Molly: Hey, how are you doing?

Liz: Me? Oh, fine. Well, no, not really, I'm a bit stressed out.

Molly: Why? Has something happened?

Liz: The shop I'm working at closed. So, I have to find a new job.

Molly: Oh dear. Well, I hope you find something soon.

Liz: Me, too. If you hear of anything, let me know.

Molly: I sure will.

Activity 2   In-Class Activity: WARM-UP

Ask your partner the following questions.

How many negative emotions can you think of?

Do you ever feel stressed?

What do you think makes people stressed?

69

'Take a deep breath' is often said when someone is angry, stressed, or upset. There is a very good reason for this advice. Have you noticed that when you are upset, your breathing becomes shallow and constricted? Your mental state and breath are connected. It can be difficult to control the mind, but we can try to control our breathing, which affects the mind. In fact, the American Institute of Stress (AIS) recommends deep breathing as a 'Super Stress Buster.' It is an effective way to promote relaxation and reduce stress by decreasing heart rate, blood pressure, and muscle tension.

Stress is a worldwide problem, and in a 2018 survey of 143 countries, the United States came 7th with 55% of people reporting feeling stressed. What is making people stressed? The most common sources of stress are work and money. The AIS lists 50 signs and symptoms of stress. The five most common are fatigue, headache, upset stomach, irritability, and feeling nervous.

Deep breathing helps to relieve stress because lengthening the exhalation activates your parasympathetic nervous system, which helps the body heal, digest food, and relax. Shallow breathing activates the sympathetic nervous system which is the part of the nervous system that prepares the body for action, to run away or deal with an emergency. It puts the body in a state of stress.

Not all stress is bad. If you have an important event or a deadline to meet, a little stress and adrenaline can help you get into action and think faster. Problems occur when the stress is chronic and that can lead to health issues.

Activity 4   VOCABULARY QUIZ

Find the right word from the essay that matches each definition below.

(1) unhappy and worried   (   )
(2) to say something or someone is good   (   )
(3) breathing out   (   )
(4) a date or time by which you have to complete something   (   )
(5) affecting a person for a long time   (   )

Activity 5   TRUE or FALSE QUESTIONS

Read the sentences and check true or false.

(1) People who are angry tend to breathe deeply.   (   )
(2) One of the most common sources of stress is money. (   )
(3) All stress is not always bad.   (   )

Activity 6   COMPREHENSION CHECK QUESTIONS

(1) What happens to your breathing when you are upset?

_____

(2) What does deep breathing activate?

_____

(3) What can a little stress and adrenaline help you do?

_____

Activity 7   WRITING

Write about how you feel when you are stressed. What do you do to stop feeling that way?

_____

_____

_____

_____

_____

(1) What do you do if you feel stressed?

_____

_____

_____

(2) What do you do when you feel sad?

_____

_____

_____

(3) What do you do if you feel angry?

_____

_____

_____

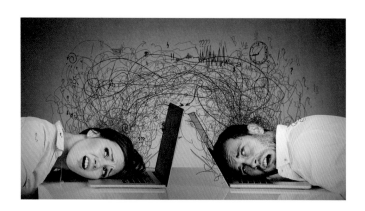

Unit 18
Ghosts

Grammar Target: Past and Present Perfect Tense

Activity 1   DIALOGUE 36

Listen and Repeat.

Eri: Have you ever seen a ghost?

Amy: No, I haven't. Have you?

Eri: Yes, I think so.

Amy: Really! What did you see?
Where did you see it?

Eri: I didn't see it clearly, but I'm sure I
saw a little girl walking along a road.

Amy: How do you know it was a ghost?

Eri: It was late at night, so I stopped my car to check if she was OK, but no
one was there.

Amy: That's scary.

Activity 2   In-Class Activity: WARM-UP

Ask your partner the following questions.

Do you like horror movies?

Do you believe ghosts exist?

Have you ever seen or felt a ghost? If yes, where were you?

Do you believe ghosts exist? 45% of Americans and 57% of Japanese people say they believe in ghosts. 18% of Americans say they have had contact with a ghost and 20% of Japanese women report having experienced the presence of a spirit. In the U.K., there are tours that take people to haunted houses for a scary experience. Many of the participants report having sensed something strange. But are there really ghosts?

New studies suggest that ghosts don't exist. They have shown that stimulation of certain brain areas can induce the feeling of a ghostly presence. Others say that fear, loneliness, and isolation could trigger changes in brain chemistry giving people a feeling of a spooky presence. In fact, lone sailors and mountain climbers in extreme situations often report the feeling that someone else was with them, perhaps guiding them out of a dangerous situation. Studies have shown that almost half of elderly widows in America have experienced the presence of their dead partner. Researchers say that this could actually be a healthy and normal way to cope with bereavement.

Another possible explanation is the power of suggestion. If the people we are with believe there are ghosts, we are more likely to sense something, too. Whatever the reason for the sensation of being in the presence of a ghost, it seems that people enjoy being afraid. Neurologists have discovered that the brain releases dopamine when we are scared. Dopamine is a brain chemical which is linked with pleasure. This could explain the popularity of horror movies and ghost stories as they give you a feeling of euphoria.

Activity 4   VOCABULARY QUIZ

Find the right word from the essay that matches each definition below.

(1) communication with a person ( )

(2) a cause for something to happen ( )

(3) strange or frightening in a way that makes you think of ghosts

( )

(4) very great in degree ( )

(5) a woman whose husband has died and who has not married again

( )

Activity 5   TRUE or FALSE QUESTIONS

Read the sentences and check true or false.

(1) More American people believe in ghosts than Japanese people. ( )

(2) Lone sailors in a dangerous situations are sometimes helped by ghosts. ( )

(3) People enjoy horror movies because of the release of dopamine in their brains.

( )

Activity 6   COMPREHENSION CHECK QUESTIONS

(1) Where does a tour in the U.K. take people?

_____

(2) What do many American widows experience?

_____

(3) What is dopamine linked with?

_____

Activity 7   WRITING

Write about a time you felt scared.

_____

_____

_____

_____

(1) Have you ever broken a bone? When …? How …?

_____

_____

_____

_____

_____

(2) Have you ever lost anything? When …? Where …?

_____

_____

_____

(3) Have you ever (your idea) …?

_____

_____

_____

Unit 19
Housing

Grammar Target: Participial Adjectives

Activity 1   DIALOGUE 38

Listen and Repeat.

Jane: Hi, I just moved into a new apartment. You must come and visit.

Luke: That's exciting. What's it like?

Jane: It has two bedrooms, a large living room and a very small kitchen.

Luke: Do you need help with anything?

Jane: No, I'm fine. Thanks. I'm just excited to have guests. Why don't you come visit me tomorrow?

Luke: OK. Give me your address and I'll come tomorrow evening.

Activity 2   In-Class Activity: WARM-UP

Ask your partner the following questions.

Where do you live?

What do you like about your room?

Would you prefer to live alone or with friends or family? Why?

It is often said that we are a product of our environment, and conversely that our environment reflects our personality. So, what does your room say about you? Are you organized? What kind of objects do you have on display? Further, the objects in our rooms can trigger certain thoughts and behaviors. For example, you are more likely to exercise if you have space to do so. Just as you are more likely to read books or study if there is a place dedicated to the activity. Pictures of friends and family will help you feel connected to them. It makes sense, to design your surroundings to suit your personality and to help you make good choices.

Two possible approaches to interior design are that of minimalism and maximalism. Minimalists believes that less is more and prefer clean lines, empty spaces, and neutral colors. It is quiet and practical with few possessions. The goal is simplicity and lightness. For minimalists this environment is relaxing. Maximalists, on the other hand, may find such emptiness boring. They tend to use bold colors, and complex patterns. They may have collections of objects which tell a story. It is usually a comfortable space with lots of furniture. Maximalists prefer their environment to be exciting and stimulating.

However, both approaches have a disregard for meaningless clutter. Clutter is considered to be made up of unnecessary items that you do not need, use, or love. If your room is messy, you will waste time looking for things. Studies have shown that people sleep better, work better, and feel less stressed in clutter-free environments. What does your room say about you, and how does it affect your daily life?

Activity 4   VOCABULARY QUIZ

Find the right word from the essay that matches each definition below.

(1) someone's character   (   )
(2) to make a plan of something that will be made   (   )
(3) having nothing inside   (   )
(4) consisting of many different parts   (   )
(5) untidy or disorganized   (   )

Activity 5   TRUE or FALSE QUESTIONS

Read the sentences and check true or false.

(1) Objects in your room affect the way you behave.   (   )
(2) Maximalists enjoy a lot of empty space for their activities.   (   )
(3) Clutter often gives people time to think deeply.   (   )

Activity 6   COMPREHENSION CHECK QUESTIONS

(1) What do photos of your friends help you do?

_____

(2) What are the goals of minimalists?

_____

(3) What will you do if your room is messy?

_____

Activity 7   WRITING

Describe your room. Write about what you like and dislike about it.

_____

_____

_____

_____

_____

(1) Is your room tidy or messy? What could you do to improve it?

_____

_____

(2) How do you feel when you are in your room?

_____

_____

(3) Are you a minimalist or a maximalist?

_____

_____

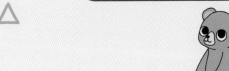

Unit 20
Gender Equality

Grammar Target: Indirect Questions

Listen and Repeat.

Kenji: So, how is life as a new dad?

Toshi: Great. I'm really enjoying spending time with my daughter.

Kenji: How is Joy doing?

Toshi: She's good. She went back to work last week. So she is tired.

Kenji: Really? So, who is looking after the baby?

Toshi: I am. I asked my boss if I could take paternity leave. My company is really good about it. I'm happy to stay at home. I've always wanted to be a house husband.

Kenji: Will you go back to work?

Toshi: Yes, we'll put our daughter into day care next year.

Activity 2   In-Class Activity: WARM-UP

Ask your partner the following questions.

Did both or one of your parents work?

How was the housework divided in your family?

Were boys and girls treated the same when you were at school?

In 1968, 187 female sewing machinists walked out of the Ford car factory in Dagenham, London. They went on strike for three weeks to protest a cut in their pay which meant they would get less pay for their skilled jobs than unskilled men. They demanded equal pay for equal work. Their action led to
5 the introduction of the Equal Pay Act in 1970, which became law in 1975.

Even though equal pay for equal work has been achieved in law, there is still inequality between men and women in the workplace. This is called the gender pay gap. The gap is calculated by taking the average hourly wage for all men in a company, and the average hourly wage for all women in a company and seeing
10 what the difference is. Among developed countries the highest gender pay gap can be seen in Korea at 37% and the lowest can be seen in Luxemburg at 3%. The gender pay gap in the U.K. is 18% and 26% in Japan.

Some reasons for the gap are that men tend to pursue higher paying jobs, so it is suggested that women should be encouraged to apply for more senior
15 roles. Also, women are often responsible for childcare and household work, so companies should make flexible work and part time work available at all levels. Another way is to encourage men to take paternity leave and to divide household and childcare duties evenly. In Japan fathers can take up to a year off for paternity leave, but only 3% of men do so. It seems that there is still plenty
20 of room for change in societal attitudes towards gender roles.

Activity 4   VOCABULARY QUIZ

Find the right word from the essay that matches each definition below.

(1) to publicly express opposition to something   (   )

(2) an unfair situation   (   )

(3) money you earn that is paid according to the amount of time you work

(   )

(4) the fact of being a father of a particular child   (   )

(5) something that you have to do as part of your job   (   )

Activity 5   TRUE or FALSE QUESTIONS

Read the sentences and check true or false.

(1) 187 women in Ford car factory fought against The Equal Pay Act.   (   )

(2) Paternity leave should be taken more by men.   (   )

(3) Japan has a long way to go to achieve gender equality.   (   )

Activity 6   COMPREHENSION CHECK QUESTIONS

(1) Why did the women in Ford factory in Dagenham go on strike?

_____

(2) What county has the lowest gender pay gap?

_____

(3) How long can fathers take paternity leave in Japan?

_____

Activity 7   WRITING

In what ways are men and women expected to behave differently? What do you think about this?

_____

_____

_____

_____

(1) What do you think about the way women are shown on Japanese TV?

_____

_____

_____

(2) Should men take paternity leave, too? Why? Why not?

_____

_____

_____

(3) If you get married and have children, would you like to stay home and take care of them? Why? Why not?

_____

_____

_____

NOTE

NOTE

Companion to English Communication

Copyright © 2021
By
Esther WAER   UCHIDA Masakatsu   KAMEYAMA Hiroyuki

著作権法上、無断複写・複製は禁じられています。

Companion to English Communication	[B-924]
大学生のための英語コミュニケーション入門	

1 刷	2021 年 1 月 30 日
2 刷	2023 年 3 月 31 日

著　者	Esther WAER	エスタ・ウェア
	内田　雅克	UCHIDA Masakatsu
	亀山　博之	KAMEYAMA Hiroyuki

発行者	南雲　一範　Kazunori Nagumo
発行所	株式会社　南雲堂
	〒162-0801　東京都新宿区山吹町361
	NAN'UN-DO Co., Ltd.
	361 Yamabuki-cho, Shinjuku-ku, Tokyo 162-0801, Japan
	振替口座：00160-0-46863
	TEL:　03-3268-2311（営業部：学校関係）
	03-3268-2384（営業部：書店関係）
	03-3268-2387（編集部）
	FAX:　03-3269-2486

編集者	加藤　敦
組　版	中西　史子
装　丁	奥定　泰之
イラスト	菊池　ひかり
検　印	省　略
コード	ISBN978-4-523-17924-5　C0082

Printed in Japan

E-mail : nanundo@post.email.ne.jp
URL : http://www.nanun-do.co.jp/